ALL
IN THE
FAMILY

ALL
IN THE
FAMILY

A Collection of Poems

Compiled by John Foster

Oxford University Press

New York   Toronto   Melbourne

Oxford University Press, Walton Street, Oxford OX2 6DP

Oxford   New York   Toronto
Delhi   Bombay   Calcutta   Madras   Karachi
Kuala Lumpur   Singapore   Hong Kong   Tokyo
Nairobi   Dar es Salaam   Cape Town
Melbourne   Auckland   Madrid

and associated companies in
Berlin   Ibadan

Oxford is a trade mark of Oxford University Press

Copyright © John Foster 1993
First published 1993

ISBN 0 19 276118 8 (hardback)
ISBN 0 19 276119 6 (paperback)

Illustrations by Michael Charlton

A CIP catalogue record for this book is available
from the British Library

Typeset in Berling by Pentacor PLC, High Wycombe, Bucks
Printed in Hong Kong

Contents

AND WHO GETS BLAMED?

WHEN I WAS YOUR AGE

HUGGER MUGGER

Beginnings

In the beginning
was one.
Crouched in a cave
where bats first hung,
where webs were first woven,
dreams first spun,
crouched one,
alone.

And then one day
into the gloom
another came;
the fire was lit
the cave was warmed,
the howl of the wind
became a song
and two
were one.

Soon winter passed,
and into the sun
from the dark of the cave
one summer dawn
crept three:
the third was a child in arms,
the three were

> *a family*, new-born.

Judith Nicholls

I TOLD YOU SO

Special Request

The day Mum had a record request on the radio
she was in the kitchen
putting the washing on.
We called her
and called her
and called her,
but all she said was,
'Turn that radio down!
I can't hear what you're saying.'
So we shouted again
as loud as we could
and in the end she came
just as the record was finishing.
'That's my favourite song,'
she said.
'Why didn't you call me?'
So we explained.
She's still not sure whether to believe us
or not.
'Me?' she said. 'Me?
A record for me?'

Brian Morse

A Parents' and Teenagers' Alphabet Book

*They're aggravating
  belly-aching
  crying out loud and always
  driving up the wall.

*They're edgy
  fractious
  grouchy and always getting on a
  high horse.

*They're insufferable
  juvenile, don't
  keep their hair on and always
  laying down the law.

*They're maddening
  never satisfied
  opinionated and always
  pointing the finger.

*They're quick-tempered
  ratty
  sulky and always ready to
  take offence.

*They're uncooperative
  very scratchy
  wearing and always e
  xtremely moody.

And
*They're unsociable and
  boring.

* *Parents/Teenagers (delete to taste)*

But those last two lines don't begin with Y and Z that's just what I'd expect
from you you can't even be bothered to find a couple of lousy words when
it's me we're talking about two words that's all I don't think you care two
hoots about my feelings you never listen anyway so what's the point in
saying anything it isn't possible to have a proper conversation with you
any more and while we're talking as a matter of fact I've got a bone to pick with you . . .

David Crystal

The Seven Commandments According to Mum

You must   Eat fish.
It's good for you.
I don't care if the bones could throttle you
and it looks like the eyes are still in.
You can always leave the skin.

You must   Wash your ears and neck.
Potatoes grow in muck.
I don't care if the soapy water runs off
your elbows and soaks your vest.
What do you mean—being nude is rude?

You must   Say 'Thank you
for having me . . . for the present'.
I don't care if you hate it at Darren's,
and bright red jumpers aren't the In thing.
At your age you shouldn't be following fashion.

16

You must	Walk the dog. It's your job. I don't care if it's raining cats as well and your wellies make your socks go to sleep. *I don't care if you haven't had your dinner yet.* You were the one wanted a pet.
You must	Be nice to your sister. She's younger than you. I don't care if she borrowed your bike without asking and poisoned your goldfish. I don't care if she did dent your bumper. You must not thump her.
You must	Honour your parents. They're your Mum and Dad. I don't care if you wish we'd never had you. I don't care if Shaun answers back all the time. That's his mother's problem. You're mine.
You must	Go to bed. You've to be up in the morning. I don't care whether it was sighing or yawning. Don't be daft—upstairs isn't cold. I couldn't care less what programme's still on. You must just do as you're told.

Jacqueline Brown

Warts and All

I've just been sent to bed,
They say I'm in disgrace
For telling Mrs Postlethwaite
She had a tickly face.

Well, she really has a warty snoz
With a muzzy just below it,
As if she's smudged her lip with soot
And pretends she doesn't know it.

She went and kissed me on the cheek
Did Mrs Whatshername:
The muzzy tickled, made me laugh.
I'm sorry she ever came.

I haven't had my supper,
I'm bored up here in bed,
And I've missed tonight's *Eastenders*
Because of what I said.

Matt Simpson

Purple Shoes

Mum and me had a row yesterday,
a big, exploding
howdareyouspeaktomelikethatI'mofftostayatGran's
kind of row.

It was about shoes.
I'd seen a pair of purple ones at Carter's,
heels not too high, soft suede, silver buckles;
'No' she said.
'Not suitable for school.
I can't afford to buy rubbish.'
That's when we had our row.

I went to bed longing for those shoes.
They made footsteps in my mind,
kicking up dance dust;
I wore them in my dreams across a shiny floor,
under flashing coloured lights.
It was ruining my life not to have them.

This morning they were mine.
Mum relented and gave me the money.
I walked out of the store wearing new purple shoes.
I kept seeing myself reflected in shop windows
with purple shoes on,
walking to the bus stop,
walking the whole length of our street
wearing purple shoes.

On Monday I shall go to school in purple shoes.
Mum will say no a thousand furious times
But I don't care.
I'm not going to give in.

Irene Rawnsley

An Embarrassing Mum

You're so embarrassing—
　　You sing in the street
　　　　You wear bright red nail polish

You shout comments so my friends
　　can hear when I'm on the phone.

You put your arm round Dad
　　—in public.

You discuss my figure
　　with the assistant in the dress shop.

You chat to babies
　　in supermarkets.

You pat me on the cheek
　　when I'm trying to tell
　　　　you something . . .

Lynette Craig

I Told You So

My mother never says, 'I told you so.'
She doesn't believe in it.
She calls it 'rubbing salt in the wound.'
But sometimes, her silences are so loud
That we wish she'd give in, for once,
And get it off our minds.

Jean Little

Growing Pains

Mother got mad at me tonight and bawled me out.
She said I was lazy and self-centred.
She said my room was a pigsty.
She said she was sick and tired of forever nagging
    but I gave her no choice.
She went on and on until I began to cry.
I hate crying in front of people. It was horrible.

I got away, though, and went to bed and it was over.
I knew things would be okay in the morning;
Stiff with being sorry, too polite, but okay.
I was glad to be by myself.

Then she came to my room and apologized.
She explained, too.
Things had gone wrong all day at the store.
She hadn't had a letter from my sister
    and she was worried.
Dad had also done something to hurt her.
She even told me about that.
Then *she* cried.
I kept saying, 'It's all right. Don't worry.'
And wishing she'd stop.

I'm just a kid.
I can forgive her getting mad at me. That's easy.
But her sadness . . .
I don't know what to do with her sadness.
I yell at her often, 'You don't understand me!'
But I don't want to have to understand her.
That's expecting too much.

Jean Little

My Dad Comes in all Shapes and Sizes

He is a tunnel of tickles,
a cave of cuddles
and the bear that lives there.

He is a mad robot
at my command (as long as
the Lego control pad holds out).

He is a wild chair
bucking and splitting, tumbling
me through the gap.

And sometimes
he is five foot six
and almost human.

John Coldwell

Lies

My father lied for me
when I refused to go to school
no special reason
except it was Monday
and raining
I blamed a headache but
he knew it wasn't true

He brought me aspirins
in a glass of water
said 'your mother would
have known what to do'
then I heard him phone
'there's been a spot of
trouble in the past

I'd like to let you know
today he's genuinely ill'
teatime he asked me
'how are you now son?'
my head was thumping from
watching videos all day
'fine' I said 'just fine'

Irene Rawnsley

in the cellar

The father is sawing, slicing the wood
with strong smooth strokes. The boy
prods a curled shaving with a chisel.

The father is concentrating; his eyes, his shoulders, his arms,
are fixed in the wood. The boy is also engrossed,
with a sharp corner he has stabbed a jagged split.

The father pauses, lays the saw on its side. What will he say?
— Now you try, hold it this way — ? or, — does that look
        straight to you — ?
No. He says — Stop fiddling. You'll spoil the chisel's point.

For what he is teaching is not woodwork, but love of making
and patience and care in the work, with the tools. And the boy
is learning about his father or perhaps about himself

and he puts the chisel back in its place
and he puts his hands in his pockets
and he tries not to lean on the wall.

Dave Calder

Over and Done With

It was an accident.
I'd told them not to
come into the yard
when she was outside.

She was asleep.
They rushed through
the gate, slamming it
into her side.

Dad wouldn't listen.
'Next time she
might not stop
at one bite.'

He rang the vet.
'I'll go,' he said.
'Get it over before you're
in from school tonight.'

Joan Poulson

Why is it?

Why is it
that when we go to the park
to fly my kite
the string always gets tangled
in the trees
and the kite gets torn
while other kids' kites
go soaring and swooping?

Why is it
that when we play cricket
on the beach
my dad always drops catches
and is out first ball,
while other kids' dads
hit the ball
over the breakwater
into the sea?

Why is it
that when my mum asks my dad
to put up a picture
on the wall,
he drills a hole
that's far too big
and gets plaster everywhere?

But when my dad
tells my brother and me stories
in the dark,
why is it
that I can almost see
the creatures
and feel their hot breath?

John Foster

Early Last Sunday Morning

Early last Sunday morning,
Dad said we needed a glass of fresh air
and a mouthful of greenness.
So off we slipped to the nearby park
where we crept in as soundless as snails.
Around us the day breathed air
that was as sharp as vinegar.
Reminding us that winter was on its way.

Inside we watched the trees stretch and wake
while the grass stood up and shivered.
Soon I was pointing towards a spider
that was strung on a necklace web.
While behind it,
the sun rolled out like a golden ball.

Dad smiled,
as a squirrel scampered from a bush
then turned to grey stone,
until with a flick of its tail
it waved goodbye and was gone.

Later as we passed the children's playground,
I looked at the lonely red slide,
and for a moment remembered the summer days
I had flown its long slippery tongue.
But a cold wind pushed me on past
until I just let the warmth in my dad's hand
lead me home.

Ian Souter

Ready, Steady? No!

My dad's
a keep-fit fiend.
You know,

press-ups and sit-ups,
jogging and squash;
toe-touch and leg-stretch,
lunch on the dash.
No time for an old-fashioned
ploughman's and beer,
'The pool's open now,
we can sprint it from here!'

Even on Sundays
he's up with the lark:
tennis in summer,
weights after dark.
Arms bend and neck twist,
runs on the spot,
scissor-jumps, rugby —
he does the lot.

As for me
I *hate* sport,
prefer bed until three;
a mere game of draughts
is exhausting to me.
He'll always hike;
well, I'll join the queue
and travel by train,
as we were meant to!

Judith Nicholls

Patterned Ways

I shall walk in my father's steps,
Not because it is easy,
But because I like the deep marks
He always makes. They are easy to follow,
Whether I trudge behind him in the snow,
Through high tall grasses, along the dunes,
Or follow him through his ploughed furrows.

When I was small, I had to stretch
My legs to match his stride.
Sometimes I failed,
But always I tried.

He shows no sign,
        nor has he ever shown a sign
He is aware of this, my following;
He sets his patterned mark for me
And filled with pride, I bravely follow him.

Now having grown a bit,
        I tread behind
With ease. Occasionally,
        (unless I watch myself),
I walk with even longer stride
And over-reach his tracks,
Make new ones of my own.

God grant that I shall mark
        a patterned way
As clear for my own son.

Jo Hilton

my dad these days

my dad takes me down the post office
the day his giro comes
to get me out from under mums feet he says
but i know he likes me to go with him

he smokes a lot in the queue
stands hunchy like hes thinking
like when him and mum
have had a barney
and hes not going to be
the next one to say nothing

when they give him the lolly
he jerks his shoulders
like as if hes glad to get it
but still he dont like taking it

on the way home he gives me a piggyback
gallops and makes a noise like a donkey
till he gets puffed

he gets more laughy
soon as hes out of the post office
he buys some fags before we get indoors
and i get a mars bar or what i like

then he gives mum most of the lolly
and she rolls her eyes up
like saying strike me is this all

dad sits hunchy more than he done
when he was up the factory
he coughs a lot and mum says
what you expect like a flaming chimney you are

then they have a barney about that
i like going down the post office with dad
but he was more laughy
when he was up the factory

Philip Guard

31

Man and Boy

'Catch the old one first,'
(My father's joke was also old, and heavy
And predictable.) 'Then the young ones
Will all follow, and Bob's your uncle.'

On slow bright river evenings, the sweet time
Made him afraid we'd take too much for granted
And so our spirits must be lightly checked.

Blessed be down-to-earth! Blessed be highs!
Blessed be the detachment of dumb love
In that broad-backed, low-set man
Who feared debt all his life, but now and then
Could make a splash like the salmon he said was
'As big as a wee pork pig by the sound of it'.

32

In earshot of the pool where the salmon jumped
Back through its own unheard concentric soundwaves
A mower leans forever on his scythe.

He has mown himself to the centre of the field
And stands in a final perfect ring
Of sunlit stubble.

'Go and tell your father,' the mower says
(He said it to my father who told me)
'I have it mowed as clean as a new sixpence.'

My father is a barefoot boy with news,
Running at eye-level with weeds and stooks
On the afternoon of his own father's death.

The open, black half of the half-door waits.
I feel much heat and hurry in the air.
I feel his legs and quick heels far away

And strange as my own — when he will piggyback me
At a great height, light-headed and thin-boned,
Like a witless elder rescued from the fire.

Seamus Heaney

What's Your Father?

At school, they used to ask me sometimes:
'What does your father do?'
(For a living, they meant.)

At first, I wanted to tell them
he was an engineer, or a steeplejack,
or an explorer, even a pop star.

But I knew they would find out
that wasn't true. I know it can't be true.
Whatever I make up about him
could never be true, because
I really don't know what he does,
or where he is, or what happened to him.

A long time ago, when I was small,
he went away, and even my mother
doesn't know where he went to —
or so she says.
(She works at the check-out counter
at the supermarket.)

Once there was a letter from him
with a foreign stamp on it.
It was from Brazil!
But I don't know what was in the letter.
My mother never showed it to me.
I watched her tear it up and burn it.
She wouldn't even let me have the stamp.
And she never speaks about him now.

I just wish he could come back one day
so I could tell them what he does.
Some of them said he must be in prison,
but I don't believe them.
And I couldn't ask my mother that sort of thing.

— But recently they've stopped asking me about him.
I wonder often if he died somewhere.
That's what it feels like now.

James Kirkup

The Pigeon

My father
with a tormented suitcase
stood at our front door
waiting for the train

that would take him
to a new house, a new wife,
a new family.
My mother

with a drowned handkerchief
lay face down on her bed
waving goodbye
to marriage.

I sat
in an attic room
bustling with departures
and people hugging each other

through jolting windows.
A solitary pigeon
perched on a high ledge
as the train pulled out.

Norman Silver

Looking for Dad

Whenever Mum and Dad
were full of gloom
they always yelled,
'TIDY UP YOUR ROOM!'
Just because my comics were
scattered here and
everywhere and
because I did not care
where I left my underwear
they yelled, 'WE'LL SEND YOU TO
A HOUSE OF CORRECTION
IF YOU DON'T TIDY UP
YOUR STAMP COLLECTION!'
Then one day they
could not care less
about the room's
awful mess.
They seemed more intent
on a domestic argument.
They both looked glum
and instead of me Dad
screeched at Mum.
One night when I
went to bed he
simply vanished.
(Ten past seven, tenth of June.)
I had not tidied
up my room because
I too was
full of gloom.
That night I dreamt
Dad was hidden
beneath the things
I'd been given.
In my dream
I was in despair

and flung about
my underwear
but could not find
him anywhere.
I looked for him
lots and lots
beneath crumpled sheets
and old robots.
I looked in cupboards
and in shoes.
I looked up all
the chimney flues.
I remembered how
he'd seemed to be
unhappier than
even me. When I woke I knew
it was not my room
that filled Mum and Dad
with so much gloom.
Now I stare at all
my old toy cars
and carpets stained
with old Mars bars
and hope he will
come back soon
and admire my very tidy room.
(It is now the twenty-ninth of June.)

Brian Patten

Without Dad

Now our Dad has left us,
It means we're only three.
There's our baby Matilda,
And of course our Mum and me.

I've thought so much about him,
Did I send Dad away?
Was it the muddle in my room,
Or the games I liked to play?

My Gran says I'm talking nonsense,
There's no way I'm to blame.
It's life that changes people,
They don't remain the same.

But I do wish things were different,
Without troubles as before.
Although we manage fairly well,
I wish that we were four.

Janet Greenyer

Mum Doesn't Live with Us Any More

There's a start of the day
Where Mum ought to be.

There's a silent breakfast
Where Mum ought to be.

There's a gate to wave at
Where Mum ought to be.

There's a coming home at four
Where Mum ought to be.

There's an empty kitchen
Where Mum ought to be.

There's an end of the day
Where Mum ought to be.

John Coldwell

Life with Father

I live alone with my father —
it's really very good
the way he copes with everything —
the wash, the shops, the food.

He's working all day long,
so it's really not much fun
if he comes home at evening
and nothing has been done.

So I try to tidy up the place
on my return from school.
You should see me in my apron —
I look a proper fool.

I vacuum the stairs and carpets,
I give the birds some seed,
I wash the breakfast dishes,
peel the vegetables we need.

I light a fire when it's cold,
I let the kettle simmer
to make a good fresh cup of tea
when he gets back for dinner.

We get along quite well, I think,
the two of us alone, you know.
But I wish my mother would come back.
I really miss her so.

We talk about her sometimes,
and I think — if she only knew,
though he says everything's OK
my father misses her too.

James Kirkup

Tug of War

My father says he loves me,
My mother says so too.
He takes me to the pictures,
She takes me to the zoo.

He buys me latest fashion clothes,
She's bought me a guitar.
He's taking me to France this year,
She's promised me a car.

He's giving me a puppy,
She buys me Chinese meals.
He asks me if I'm happy,
She wonders what I feel.

She doesn't live with father,
He doesn't live with her.
They don't talk about each other:
Their meeting won't occur.

I stand between my parents,
The red rag and the bull.
I'm just a teenage tightrope:
Can't bear the tug and pull.

John Kitching

Stepmother

My Stepmother
    is really nice.
She ought to wear
    a label.
I don't come in
    with a latch key, now —
my tea is on
    the table.
She doesn't nag at me
    or shout.
I often hear her
    singing.
I'm glad my dad
    had wedding bells —
and I hope
    they go on ringing.

Stepmothers
    in fairy tales
are hard and cold
    as iron.
There isn't a lie
    they wouldn't tell,
or a trick
    they wouldn't try on.
But MY stepmother's
    warm and true;
she's kind, and cool,
    and clever —
Yes! I've a *wicked*
    stepmother —
and I hope she stays
    for ever!

Jean Kenward

Engaged

My parents have never told Marilyn and me
How they got engaged or exactly where or when.
We've asked over and over.
They look at each other and laugh.
'Wasn't it in that restaurant,' Mother says,
    'where the gypsy played?'
'Oh, no, no! On the steamship behind the lifeboat,'
    Dad reminds her.
Then they laugh again. They make Marilyn furious.
But I like wondering
— And I like the way they laugh together,
    leaving us both outside.

Jean Little

Mama

Mama gone to market
with the figs upon her head.
She wearin' her soft blue
dress for selling
with the fish 'round the hem.
Her hair is plaited neatly
in two long straps of black.
She walkin' tall in sandals
with the bamboo beads intact.
Mama look like Christmas
with red sorrel behind her ears.
She balance her wicker basket
like the Star of Bethlehem.

Lynn Joseph

A Family Photo

This is my dad,
That's my step-mum, Irene,
And this is the baby, Annie.
That's their dog, Dozer,
He's so funny,
He always sits under the table.

No, I'm not in that picture.

Lynette Craig

She is Making a Cake

She makes it with cherries, sultanas and raisins.
She makes it with salt,
with flour and with tears.

Takes them   and weighs them
             on uneven scales
             that have always been tilted against her.

She weighs   the moments,
             the laughter,
             the pain.

She weighs   up the waiting,
             the ploys,
             and the games.

Her children ask if they can scrape the bowl.
With a great wooden spoon
              they savour the smiles,
              lick at the loving,
              the sweet golden lies.

She bakes   the smooth mixture
             in an oven of gas,
             pacing the kitchen
             as she wills it to rise.

Then her children come straggling
in from their play
to cut thick heavy slices,
still steaming and warm
which they chew over in silence
and leave her just one lonely crumb.

Dave Ward

Daydreams

My mum loved
the colour blue
and barley-sugars, rum and coke,

mustard on her kippers, bowls of tripe,
Coronation Street and TV games.
Whist and rummy, bingo, beetle drives,

a movie star with eyes like hard-boiled eggs.
Waltzing round the kitchen, singing hymns,
and shouting at my dad.

And she loved to daydream.
I can see her now, sitting by the fire,
gazing at the flames and shadows there.

Though what she saw in them I never knew
I thought her secret died along with her.
Till now. Till my dreams came.

And now I know just what it was she dreamed.
It was her own mum she could see
years ago, dreaming just like her, like me.

Berlie Doherty

Mum Dad and Me

My parents grew among palmtrees,
in sunshine strong and clear.
I grow in weather that's pale,
misty, watery or plain cold,
around back streets of London.

Dad swam in warm sea, at my age.
I swim in a roofed pool.
Mum—she still doesn't swim.

Mum went to an open village market
at my age. I go to a covered
arcade one with her now.
Dad works most Saturdays.

At my age Dad played
cricket with friends.
Mum helped her mum, or talked
shouting halfway up a hill.
Now I read or talk on the phone.

With her friends Mum's mum washed
clothes on a river-stone. Now
washing-machine washes our clothes.
We save time to eat to TV,
never speaking.

My dad longed for a freedom in Jamaica.
I want a greater freedom.
Mum prays for us, always.

Mum goes to church
some evenings and Sundays.
I go to the library.
Dad goes for his darts at the local.

Mum walked everywhere, at my age.
Dad rode a donkey.
Now I take a bus
or catch the underground train.

James Berry

Urgent Note to my Parents

Don't ask me to do what I can't do
Only ask me to do what I can
Don't ask me to be what I can't be
Only ask me to be what I am

Don't one minute say 'Be a big girl'
And the next 'You're too little for that'
PLEASE don't ask me to be where I can't be
PLEASE be happy with right where I'm at

Hiawyn Oram

My Mum

My Mum was a mince pie of a mum.
A 'doyouwantabiscuitwithyourtea?'
kind of Mum.
A roast potato
     brown gravy
     crackle on the pork
     yorkshire pud
kind of lady.

She was a
     houseful of everyone
     polish the brass
     whiten the step
     rush to the shops
     bucket and mops
kind of lady.

A — 'hello dear'
     always near
     hurry scurry
'Oh, don't worry . . .'
kind of Mum.

She collected —
     old people
     funny stories
     and other people's children.
She called everyone by an invented name
and was a champion
               bus waiter
               queuer
               visitor
               laugher
        and Nutall Mint sucker.

She was someone
who
would give anyone
her last mint.

Peter Dixon

Lost and Found

In my parents' eyes I see
The child that I was meant to be
But who's gone missing? Them or me?

And who is it owns this tangled ground
Where each of us plays lost and found
Until there's nobody around?

John Mole

AND WHO GETS BLAMED?

our baby

we've got a new baby
at our house

they call her Mandy Jane

she's fat and bald
with a line in charm
that's an absolute pain
when you've seen it all before

there's six of us now

so this new one's
got a lot of stick to come

but I reckon if anybody else
gets at her
he'd best know how to run

because
well

she's our kid sister
isn't she.

Joan Poulson

Cradle Song

Little baby sister,
Fast asleep,
If I were to poke you
Would you weep?

If I were to pinch you,
Would you yell?
Mummy wouldn't like that —
She'd give me hell.

No, I will not harm you.
Do not cry.
Darling little baby,
Hushabye.

Lulla, lulla, rock you.
What a din!
Darling little baby,
Pack it in.

Could you please stop bawling,
Just for me?
This lullaby's a failure,
I can see.

I'll be in big trouble,
Thanks to you.
Little baby sister,
Lullaboo!

Wendy Cope

New Baby

Mi baby sista come home las' week
An' little most mi dead,
When mama pull back de blanket
An' me see de pickney head.

Couple piece a hair she hab pon i',
An de little pickney face
Wrinkle up an crease up so,
It was a real disgrace.

Mi see har a chew up mama chest
So mi gi' har piece o' meat,
Mama tek i' whey, sey she cyaan eat yet
For she no hab no teeth.

Mi tell mama fi put har down
Mek she play wid me blue van,
She sey Yvonne cyaan siddung nor stan' up yet
Nor hol' tings eena har han'.

Mi sey a' right but maybe
She can play 'I spy' wid mi,
She tell mi de pickney cyaan talk yet
And she can hardly see.

Aldoah she no hab no use,
An she always wet har bed,
Mi wouldn' mine so much ef she neva
Mek so much nize a mi head.

Every night she wake mi up;
But a mama mi sorry fah,
For everytime she wake up
She start fi eat mama.

She blind, she dumb, she ugly, she bald,
She smelly, she cyaan understan',
A wish mama would tek har back
An' buy one different one.

Valerie Bloom

My little sister

My little sister
Likes to eat.
But when she does
She's not too neat.
The trouble is
She doesn't know
Exactly where
The food should go!

William Wise

And Who Gets Blamed?

My younger brother
Is a real trickster;
He's always got
Something up his sleeve —

Like showing me
How to make
A litre of ice cream
Disappear in a flash,
And then, as if by magic,
Vanishing himself
When our mum arrives —
Leaving me
With my hands
Still clutching
The empty container.

Some trick, eh?

Trevor Harvey

Snaps

One: just a year
a plump and smiling cherub
posed naked
on a cushion
bottom up

Two: proud sister
of new twins
one in each arm
no jealousy
all smiles
still after all
first come

Three: arms spread wide
bare feet
on new-mown lawn
still smiling
topped with curls
a back-garden
princess

Four: time for
the dancing show
a dressed-up doll
gingham and frills
wide lipstick smile
huge ribbon
over all

Five: seaside scene
among the sandwiches
the smiling
queen of the castle
spade aloft
bossing the twins
flags flying

Six: taller now
and all in
navy-blue
a satchel strap
dragging a shoulder
down
curls caught
in a basin hat   Smile please

Anne Harvey

Life According to my Brother

I've had it
I've really had it
And I've said so to my mother
I'm sick of it
Completely sick of it
Life According to my Brother

When Ben wants to listen to HIS tapes
What do we listen to? Of course
And when I sing along to pass the time
He hits me for singing hoarse

When Ben wants the yellow whatever
Not the green one that he first chose
My dad makes me give him MY yellow one
Because of the tantrums he throws

Well, I've had it
I've really had it
Living Life According to Ben
And I'm off
To the bottom of the garden
And I'm not coming back till he's ten

Hiawyn Oram

Sharing

My mother used to say —
you lot have got to learn to share.
But there were five of us
and if you shared
you never ended up with much.
My older brother Tom
hoarded sweets,
forgetting where he'd stored them.
You'd come across forgotten treats,
mouldy packets of Polos
chocolate turned a funny colour,
winegums that swarmed with ants.
But I would eat sweets
as quickly as I could,
in case I was made to share.
I'd cram my mouth
till my cheeks puffed out
like a hamster's pouch.
My other brothers shared theirs out.
When I'd finished mine
I would sit on the stairs
and watch them eat theirs,
sucking pear drops,
chewing toffees that were tasty,
and wish I hadn't been so hasty.

Pie Corbett

Birthdays

When I was six
Everyone had birthday parties.
We always had Dead Lions,
Musical Bumps, Being Sick
And Pass the Parcel . . .

Between each wrapper
Round the swollen present
Lay tucked a toffee
Or a lollipop —
And everybody got a turn
At taking off a layer.

When I was nine, I learned
That the way the music stopped
Was not by chance:
My father's gaze took in
Each trembling lip, each face,
Each pair of hopeful eyes.

When I was twelve, I realized
With some surprise
That later on in life
There's no one there
To press the switch
And make sure
That everything is fair
And everybody
Gets their
Share.

Trevor Millum

Sarah, My Sister, has Asthma

Sarah, my sister, has asthma.
Sometimes, I wake up in the night
And hear her wheezing
In the bunk below.

I remember the time
I woke to hear her gasping for breath
And Mum had to call an ambulance.
They took her to the hospital
And kept her in for tests.

'She's allergic,' the doctor said.
'I expect she'll grow out of it.
Most young children do.'

Now she carries an inhaler
Everywhere she goes.

She gets annoyed when people
Try to stop her doing things.
She's always telling Grandma
To stop fussing.

'I'm not different,' she says.
'It's only asthma.
Lots of people have it.'

On Sports Day
Sarah came first in the high jump.
'You see, I'm not different,' she said.

Sarah, my sister, has asthma.
Sometimes I wake up in the night
And hear her wheezing
In the bunk below.

John Foster

Harry Pushed Her

Harry pushed her;
He pushed her around;
He pushed his sister.
Before school, after school;
On weekends.
He pushed his sister;
He had no friends.
He pushed her — school-holidays
And Christmas time.
The children always
Sang their made-up rhyme:
'Harry push her, push her now!
Harry push the crazy cow!'
Harry pushed her without strain:
Through snow, sunshine, wind and rain.
She smiled strangely
And never said a word.
He pushed her for years —
It was so absurd.
Harry was twelve;
His sister twenty-three.
Harry never had a childhood like me.
Harry pushed her without a care;
He pushed his sister in her wheelchair.

Peter Thabit Jones

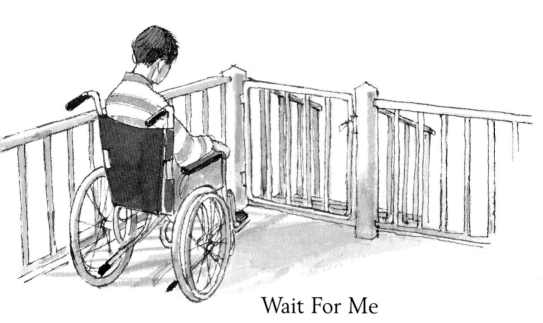

Wait For Me

My brother Tim
Is three years older than me.

When I was six,
I could never keep up with him.
I remember
Running down the path after him
Shouting, 'Wait for me!
Wait for me!'

Since the accident,
Tim can't run any more.
Now, he sits in his chair,
Waiting for me
As I hurry on ahead
To open the gate
And help him down the steps.

John Foster

TV Soap Addict

If there's one thing my sister likes
It's *Neighbours*.
Not as much as
Coronation Street
But better than
Eastenders except at
Tea-time when she
Usually watches
Home and Away
And my dad shouts
'Turn that telly off will you
And come and have your tea!'
And she
Goes 'Just a minute
He's just going to
Kiss her!' and Dad says
'Never mind that — your
Tea's getting cold!'
And Mum says 'Don't shout, dear,
It's only a bit of escapism!'
Then Dad says 'Escapism be blowed!
She ought to be thinking about
Real Life!'
Then my sister comes in
And she goes
'Real life?
    …What's that?'

Irene Yates

Listn Big Brodda Dread, Na!

My sista is younga than me.
My sista outsmart five-foot three.
My sista is own car repairer
and yu nah catch me doin judo with her.

> I sey I wohn get a complex.
> I wohn get a complex.
> Then I see the muscles my sista flex.

My sista is tops at disco dance.
My sista is well into self-reliance.
My sista plays guitar and drums
and wahn see her knock back double rums.

> I sey I wohn get a complex.
> I wohn get a complex.
> Then I see the muscles my sista flex.

My sista doesn mind smears of grease and dirt.
My sista'll reduce yu with sheer muscle hurt.
My sista says no guy goin keep her phone-bound —
with own car mi sista is a wheel-hound.

> I sey I wohn get a complex.
> I wohn get a complex.
> Then I see the muscles my sista flex.

James Berry

Sister in a Whale

You live in the hollow of a stranded whale
lying on top of our house.
My father was embarrassed by this
so a roof was put up as camouflage.
On the ribs you have hung plants
and a miniature replica of a whale
to remind you where you are.
The stomach lining is plastered with posters
and your *Snoopy for President* buttons
are stuck to a piece of blubber beside your bed.
Through the spout you observe cloud formations.
It isn't as orderly as a regular room:
it's more like a shipwreck of notebooks,
school projects, shirts, paper bags,
coke cans, photographs and magazines
that has been washed up with the tide.
You beachcomb every morning for something to wear;
then it's down the corkscrew
to the real world.

Julie O'Callaghan

68

69

Smart Remark

When my older sister Marilyn came for a visit,
She spent most of her time trying to make us over
Into some other kind of family.
The kind you see on TV who get all excited and beam
Because they're having Lipton's Chicken Noodle soup
      for supper.
The kind who pick to spend the whole day in the new Mall.
The kind who love to do things together and talk non-stop.
The kind we aren't.

When she said, for the fifteenth time,
'Kate, must you always have your head in a book?'
The worm turned and I snapped, 'Yes. I must.
It's better than having no head
— Like you!'

Dad laughed.
Mother sent me to my room.

Afterwards, she said,
'It was clever, Kate. It may even have been true.
But you didn't have to hurt her.'

'She hurt *me*!' I complained.
'Did she really?' Mother asked, looking at me in the eye.
'Oh, I guess not,' I said, thinking back over the visit.
'But she drove me crazy, picking at me . . . and . . .'

'You wanted to swat her,' Mother finished for me.
'So did we all. But you don't swat butterflies, Kate.'
'If she's a butterfly, what am I?' I demanded.
'A mosquito,' my father joined in.
'But Marilyn's not exactly a butterfly, April.
She's more like a . . . tent caterpillar.'

Mother laughed.
Why didn't she send *him* to his room?

I know why.
He said it when Marilyn couldn't hear.
In other words, behind her back.
Which makes him a spider?

And Mother . . . a . . . a . . .
Queen Bee, I suppose.

Jean Little

Why Is It?

Why is it,
That,
In our bathroom,
It's not the dirtiest
Or the strongest
Who stay longest?
BUT
It always seems to be
The one who gets there
Just ahead
Of me.

Why is it
That people fret
When they're wet,
With loud cries
And soap in their eyes
And agonized howls,
Because they forget
Their towels?

Why is it that —
When *I'm* in the bath,
Steaming and dreaming,
My toes just showing
And the hot water flowing,
That other people
Yell and say,
'Are you there to stay
Or just on a visit?'

Why is it?

Max Fatchen

My Foster Brother

My foster brother
had spiky hair
and a long white scar
on the crown of his head.
On the day he came
he sat in the kitchen
with his shoulders hunched
and glared at us all
through thick, round glasses.
He reminded me
of a baby owl —
except he wasn't
sweet and fluffy.

He stole my gold cross.
He smoked fags, leaning
out of the window
when Dad wasn't looking.
He tormented the cat.
He kicked my sister
into a gorse bush.
He had us looking
over our shoulders
all the time and
he wanted my mum
and dad to himself.
I thought I hated him —
until he ran away.

Jennifer Tweedie

Oh, Brother!

My brother's a motorbike freak.
Each week,
He rides races
In the oddest places.
He climbs hills,
Has spills.
He speeds
And cruises.
He gets action,
Satisfaction,
But mostly,
He gets bruises.

Max Fatchen

stars

in science today we learned
that stars are a mass of gases that burned
out a long time ago only we don't know
that because we still see the glow

and i remembered my big brother donny
said he burned out a long time ago and i asked
him did that make him
a star

Nikki Giovanni

WHEN I WAS YOUR AGE

A Thoroughly Modern Grandmama

I've become a world authority
on how grandmothers *ought* to look
because dotty dear old ladies
smile from every picture book.

They're usually round and cuddly
with grey hair and a hat.
They drink endless cups of milky tea,
always, always have a cat.

They are very good at knitting
and they'll mind you for the day —
I'm sure picture book grannies are
all very well, but boring in their way.

Now *my* grandmother hasn't read
the books — she hasn't got a clue
about the way she should behave
and the things she mustn't do.

She's always on a diet
and I'm sure she dyes her hair,
and I haven't got a grandpapa so
her boyfriend's sometimes there.

She wears jazzy shirts and skin-tight
jeans, jangles bracelets on her arm.
She zooms me around in her little car,
strapped-in, and safe from harm.

She's a busy lady with a job
and a diary to book me in.
She doesn't knit and doesn't drink tea,
preferring coffee, wine or gin!

My grandmother's a complete disaster
as ordinary grannies go —
but I wouldn't want to swap her
or I'd have done it long ago!

Moira Andrew

my Gran

her forehead's finely crackled
like an old china cup
lips neatly pleated
and pin-tucked
blue eyes
like bright beads
peep out beneath white brows
her snowy hair
fits smoothly as a cap

living more in yesterday
she watches time fly by
the present
is a minefield she mistrusts
her territory has slowly shrunk
to one small battered base
a fox-hole
where she sits and waits
a sanctuary of dreams.

Joan Poulson

Gran Can You Rap?

Gran was in her chair she was taking a nap
When I tapped her on the shoulder to see if she could rap.
Gran, can you rap? Can you rap? Can you, Gran?
And she opened one eye and said to me, man,
    I'm the best rapping Gran this world's ever seen
    I'm a tip-top, slip-slap, rap-rap queen.

And she rose from her chair in the corner of the room
And she started to rap with a bim-bam-boom,
And she rolled up her eyes and she rolled round her head
And as she rolled by this is what she said,
    I'm the best rapping Gran this world's ever seen
    I'm a nip-nap, yip-yap, rap-rap queen.

Then she rapped past my dad and she rapped past my mother,
She rapped past me and my little baby brother.
She rapped her arms narrow she rapped her arms wide,
She rapped through the door and she rapped outside.
    She's the best rapping Gran this world's ever seen
    She's a drip-drop, trip-trap, rap-rap queen.

She rapped down the garden she rapped down the street,
The neighbours all cheered and they tapped their feet.
She rapped through the traffic lights as they turned red
As she rapped round the corner this is what she said,
    I'm the best rapping Gran this world's ever seen
    I'm a flip-flop, hip-hop, rap-rap queen.

She rapped down the lane she rapped up the hill,
And as she disappeared she was rapping still.
I could hear Gran's voice saying, Listen, man,
Listen to the rapping of the rap-rap Gran.
    I'm the best rapping Gran this world's ever seen
    I'm a —
        tip-top, slip-slap,
          nip-nap, yip-yap,
            hip-hop, trip-trap,
              touch yer cap,
                take a nap,
                  happy, happy, happy, happy,
                rap — rap — queen.

Jack Ousbey

Grandfather

my grandfather's eyes
are sea fog grey.
his face is scribbled
like a little sister's sketch,
his arms marked
like a giraffe.
my grandfather's voice
is a chirping bird
in a sunset nest.
hands that carved kraal patterns
on boxes and bowls
shake like shivering children.
he carved this whistle bird
at the end of an ox thong
round my neck.
grandfather's smell
is tobacco earth
ripe for reaping.
he sits sun-trapped
in pants wide
like water pipes —
specials from the trading store.
and if you bring him
ten cents tobacco,
he'll smile a crescent moon,
and chirp a tale
of how he walked
ten miles to school,
carved a kudu horn
for the Fathers,
cried when granny died,
how as a young man
sun ripe,
he saw the seasons.

Dorian Haarhoff

Grandpa

Sundays Grandpa sleeps on his hand —
in the armchair, belt off;
breathing like
when he cools his tea,
all blow and suck.

Time for my balloon game.
How near can I get
without touching?
Then, how many times
tag, not wake him?

There it goes, on to
his bald head,
dances softly over his stomach
— one, two (thigh and knee) —
then down to his feet (they're big as blocks).

When I've played enough
I let it out.
Whoosh, away it snorts —
biffs the ceiling,
collapses — whack.

And he turns on his hand,
grunts 'You again!';
clamps his eyes,
goes snoring off . . .
louder than Mum's new vac.

Geoffrey Holloway

Grandpa

blossoms
out and up
over the weary waistband
of his trunks
(they must have seen
a hundred years of wear!)
knots his frayed hankie
like a parachute
to cover fraying hair
then eases down.
In less than half an hour
the *Sunday Mail* has slipped,
its rustle masking
Grandpa's gentle snore.
Sun and the journey,
age and the salt-sea air
return him to an earlier trip
(*When I was young . . .*)
The paper crumples,
slides to the sand
beneath his bulging chair.
Softly he sighs for summers lost;
snores loudly into sleep,
then settles dreams and flesh
more deeply in the canvas,
layer by layer.

Judith Nicholls

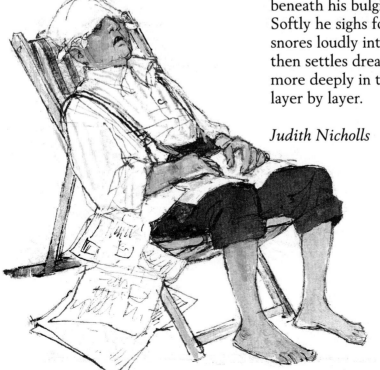

Child with a Cause

My grandmother was chicken-plump.
She wore long earrings, smelled of
Pear's soap and lavender water.
She kept cream in a jug under
a blue-beaded net.

Grandfather kept us both
on a tight rein, our place
at the kitchen sink. When Gran's mind
slipped slightly out of gear
I was her memory.

Nearly always, that is. She peeled
potatoes once, put them ready
for Grandfather's tea and forgot
to light the gas. He was furious.
I saw Gran's tears.

Upstairs, in the narrow hall
I waited, scuffing the turkey-red rug.
He took his time. The flush thundered.
His shape vultured against
the door. I was raw

as carrion. 'It's not fair.
You made Gran cry.' He lunged at me.
'How dare you, child? How dare you
speak to me like that?' Picked clean
by anger I ran.

'Don't mind him,' my grandmother said.
'He likes his tea on time.' The matter
was closed. Grandfather tore into
his beef stew and mashed potatoes.
I pushed my plate away.

Moira Andrew

'You're Right,' Said Grandad

I went round to help him
the day he moved
it was an upstairs flat
this old one he had
he'd lived there
with Gran
for twenty-nine years
they told him
it was time
he had a move.

we laughed, me and Grandad
at the dark front room
'Like an old fox's den,'
I said. 'Just wait until
you're sitting in that bright
light room — with all
that glass. You'll be able to
sit and watch
everybody pass.'
'You're right, I will,'
said Grandad.

we laughed, me and Grandad
at the garden round the back.
'Like a jungle, at its best,'
I said. 'Just wait until
you're resting in your
new place. No more
hacking-out
a deckchair space.
No weeds annoying you.
There'll be plenty
company for you, too.

They'll sit outside
the people from
the other bungalows
sit on the benches
chat with you.'
'You're right, they will,'
said Grandad.

we laughed, me and Grandad
at his rickety old shed.
'Like something from
a horror film!' I said.
'You'll be much better off
without it. And didn't
the doctor tell you
all that sawdust
wasn't good, got on your chest?
And we've all got wooden stools
and things, enough to last
a lifetime, anyway.
Our Sheryll really loved
that box you made her.
All those different
colours, different woods.
Dad says you've been a
first-rate craftsman
in your time.'
'He's right, I have,'
said Grandad.
'Yes, I have.'

Joan Poulson

When I was Your Age

When I was your age,
My grandad, who was
Older then than I am now,
And I'm nearly fifty,
He used to say to me,
'You don't know what
Hard work is!'

He used to say,
'When I was your age,
Every morning,
Before I could go to school,
I used to have to do
A full paper round.

'But,

'Before I could do
My paper round, I had to
Clean all the shoes
For my brothers and sisters.

'But,

'Before that, I had to
Clean out the grate,
Take the ashes out to the yard,
Fill the coal scuttle,
Make paper spills,
And lay the fire,
So that all my
Mother had to do was
Put a match to it
When she got up to make
Our breakfast,
Which was always
A piece of dip and bread,
Which you ate on your way
To school, or you'd be
Late otherwise.

'But,

'Before I could lay the fire,
I had to take the milk bottle
Out to the step,
And leave it, with the token
Under it, for the milkman
When he called, which was always
While I was out,
Doing my paper round.

'I'm telling you,'
He used to tell me,
'When I was your age,
I had so much to do
Every morning,
Before I went to school,
I used to have to get up
Before I went to bed!'

2

When I was your age,
My grandad used to say
'You kids of today,
You don't know you're born.'

I once asked my mam.
I said 'Mam, am I born?'
She said 'What are you
On about?'

I said 'My grandad said . . .'
She said 'What did he say?'
I said 'He said
"I don't know I'm born." '
She said 'You want to take
No notice of him,' she said.
'He talks a lot of nonsense.'

John Bond

Gapping the Generations

'When I went to school
our desks were in rows,
and when the master came in
we stood up and said *Sir!*'
my grandfather said.

'So did we,' said my father.

'We wrote with dip-in pens
in copper-plate,
and got caned if we blotted
our copy-book,'
my grandfather said.

'More or less the same,
except we had fountains,'
said my father.

'We had respect for our elders,
none of this questioning authority,
none of this ducking responsibility.
We looked people in the eye,'
my grandfather said.

'We muttered occasionally,'
said my father.
'Otherwise ditto.'

'No long-haired hippies.
No CND marches.
No rock-and-roll rubbish.
No demonstrations against apartheid.
None of this everyone equal —'

'Hey!' my father said.
'That's us you're talking about!
Not this lot!
You're twenty years out of date!
You've got the wrong generation!
Silly old goat!'

Brian Morse

Names

She was Eliza for a few weeks
When she was a baby —
Eliza Lily. Soon it changed to Lil.

Later she was Miss Steward in the baker's shop
And then 'my love', 'my darling', Mother.

Widowed at thirty, she went back to work
As Mrs Hand. Her daughter grew up,
Married and gave birth.

Now she was Nanna. 'Everybody
Calls me Nanna,' she would say to visitors.
And so they did — friends, tradesmen, the doctor.

In the geriatric ward
They used the patients' Christian names.
'Lil,' we said, 'or Nanna.'
But it wasn't in her file
And for those last bewildered weeks
She was Eliza once again.

Wendy Cope

Great-Grandad

Great-Grandad forgets
The time of the day,
Where he was going,
What he wanted to say.

Great-Grandad forgets
The day of the week.
He cannot recall
What we say when we speak.

Great-Grandad forgets
What he wants to do.
Sometimes when he sees me
He thinks that I'm you.

But Great-Grandad remembers
The relief and delight
The day the war ended
And they partied all night.

Great-Grandad remembers
How as a young man
He first met the girl
Who is now our Great-Gran.

Great-Grandad remembers
How things used to be
And I smile as he tells
His memories to me.

John Foster

We Went to See Our Gran Today

We went to see our Gran today,
we went to see our Gran;
in the big white-clean hospital
where the nurses smile
and speak in soft voices.

We went to see our Gran today,
we went to see our Gran,
in the big sunshiney room
where the old people sit in chairs
and say nothing to the television.

We went to see our Gran today,
we went to see our Gran,
in the little room with the shiny metal things
and the big white curtains.
I showed her my drawing of our cat in the rain,
and it made her cry.

We went to see our Gran today,
we went to see our Gran;
but today she didn't say anything,
she didn't even say hello,
she just smiled
and her eyes were bright.

We went to see our Gran today,
we went to see our Gran,
in the dark room next to the doctor's.
She was sleeping,
and her hands were cold,
and the nurses were very quiet
and quickly drew the curtains.

Christopher Mann

Tomorrow is Another Day

She left the kitchen tidy.
The rhubarb was in the pan
all cut up and ready to go.
I lifted the lid. The blanket
of sugar was red as Burgundy.

They had dressed Gran
in a cotton gown, the pink
eiderdown drawn up to her
chin. Cold, she was, all
living colour drained away.

Cotton wool wisped from
her lips. I longed to tuck
it in, to leave her looking
tidy. Her motto was to be
ready for every eventuality.

Clean knickers, will be in
the top drawer, white nightgown
wrapped in tissue paper.
She'd even wakened Grandpa
to tell him she was going.

'Phone Dolly,' she'd said,
organizing the family to the
end. 'She'll find everything
ready for tomorrow's lunch.
Cold roast, rhubarb in the pan.'

Moira Andrew

Allotment Rose

Why are you sighing — dear Grandad
and why are you smelling that rose?
Why is it special — dear Grandad
and why do your eyelashes close?

What do its words say — dear Grandad
on the stick with the bright orange band?
What are you thinking of — Grandad
and why are you squeezing my hand?

Peter Dixon

Grandad

Grandad's dead
And I'm sorry about that.

> He'd a huge black overcoat.
> He felt proud in it.
> You could have hidden
> A football crowd in it.
> Far too big —
> It was a lousy fit
> But Grandad didn't
> Mind a bit.
> He wore it all winter
> With a squashed black hat.

Now he's dead
And I'm sorry about that.

> He'd got twelve stories.
> I'd heard every one of them
> Hundreds of times
> But that was the fun of them:
> You knew what was coming
> So you could join in.
> He'd got big hands
> And brown, grooved skin
> And when he laughed
> It knocked you flat.

Now he's dead
And I'm sorry about that.

Kit Wright

Newcomers

My father came to England
from another country
my father's mother came to England
from another country
but my father's father
stayed behind.

So my dad had no dad here
and I never saw him at all.

One day in spring
some things arrived:
a few old papers,
a few old photos
and — oh yes —
a hulky bulky thick checked jacket
that belonged to the man
I would have called 'Grandad'.
The Man Who Stayed Behind.
But I kept that jacket
and I wore it
and I wore it
and I wore it
till it wore right through
at the back.

Michael Rosen

The Older the Violin the Sweeter the Tune

Me Granny old
Me Granny wise
stories shine like a moon
from inside she eyes.

Me Granny can dance
Me Granny can sing
but she can't play the violin.

Yet she always saying,
'Dih older dih violin
de sweeter de tune.'

Me Granny must be wiser
than the man inside the moon.

John Agard

Croglofft Cottage

When I was young
and chin high to the table top,
I looked up at everything.

The two rooms
of my grandparents' dwelling
were flag floored, boulder walled

and up into the ceiling hole
was that ladder
which led to heaven.

My grandad told me so.

'That's where we climb to sleep
your gran and me.
In the loft we're in heaven —
you're too young to go up there.'

It was a dark void
and now and then
an unsure place
of candle-made flickering
angel-shapes
as my gran moved
slowly to and fro.

Years later, after they had died,
I returned.
Bramble thorns caught my coat
as I clambered over rubble.
Windows were smashed,
the front door had gone
and I looked up
through rotting laths
and could see the sky.

The roof of heaven
had fallen in.

I had hoped
but couldn't even find
a fallen angel's wing.

David Watkin Price

The Picture

There's a picture that my dad's got,
　　He keeps it by his bed,
Of him when he was little,
　　With my grandpa, who's dead.

They're standing close together,
　　On a day out at the fair;
Grandpa's got his arm round Dad.
　　No one else is there.

Both of them are smiling,
　　And looking straight ahead;
My dad with his father,
　　With my grandpa, who's dead.

I never knew my grandpa,
　　And he never knew of me,
But even though we didn't meet
　　We're still family.

Dad looks just like Grandpa,
　　And I'm like Dad, Mum said;
Which means I look like Grandpa,
　　My grandpa, who's dead.

They're happy in that picture,
　　On a day out at the fair;
And I know it's strange to say it,
　　But I wish that I'd been there.

There before the camera,
　　Looking straight ahead,
With my dad when he was little,
　　And my grandpa, who's dead.

Tony Bradman

HUGGER MUGGER

My Relations

Somebody knitted my aunt Julia,
started at the bobble on her blue wool hat,
needles clicking like ancient false teeth,
to the tips of her woolly toes.

She was popped through the door
of the cold, old house
where she lives today, without a budgie
or even a mouse for company.

Uncle Frisco was made by a Swiss toymaker
who took a month to put him together,
to paint his buttoned coat and shiny boots,
the parting in his hair.

He was wound up and set free in the street;
he came to rest at a bus stop
where he stood tut tut tutting
because the bus was late.

A Master Chef created Auntie Amber
He decided for fun to shape a face
on an apple dumpling,
shiny currant eyes and a wide smile.

He baked her slowly in a warm oven
until she came out smelling delicious
with a powdery dust of flour on the pastry,
so nice he couldn't bear to eat her.

Irene Rawnsley

My Aunt

I take my Aunt out in her pram
I am her grown-up Nephew 'Sam'!
My Grandma's sister married late
And by a stroke of Life's strange fate
Her children all arrived when we
Were roundabout aged Twenty-three.
It is most pleasing for a chap
To bounce his Aunt upon his lap!

Peggy Wood

Aunt Lavinia

Aunt Lavinia is the one
we never see
she keeps her address
a mystery
she's waiting for the
right clothes and a
house she's proud of
I wish she understood
about love

Eloise Greenfield

Indian Wedding

Tomorrow
My aunt's wedding.
So excited I hardly sleep.
Morning —
Get up
Have a bath
Put on my blue lenga
With matching dupatta.
The bride wears a red, shiny saree
With lots of jewellery and make-up.
She sits on a very special chair
As the priest says the wedding prayers.
Everybody is happy —
Dancing
Celebrating
Eating the food.
Maybe one day it will be me.

Sapna Rehan

Hugger Mugger

I'd sooner be
Jumped and thumped and dumped,

I'd sooner be
Slugged and mugged . . . than *hugged*

And clobbered with a slobbering
Kiss by my Auntie Jean:

You know what I mean:

Whenever she comes to stay,
You know you're bound

To get one.
A quick
   short
   peck
   would
   be
   OK.
But this is a
Whacking great
Smacking great
Wet one!

All whoosh and spit
And crunch and squeeze
And '*Dear* little boy!'
And 'Auntie's missed you!'
And 'Come to Auntie, she
Hasn't *kissed* you!'
Please don't do it, Auntie,
PLEASE!

Or if you've absolutely
Got to,

And nothing on *earth* can persuade you
Not to,

The trick
Is to make it
Quick,

You know what I mean?

For as things are,
I really would far,

Far sooner be
Jumped and thumped and dumped,

I'd sooner be
Slugged and mugged . . . than *hugged* . . .

And clobbered with a slobbering
Kiss by my Auntie

Jean!

Kit Wright

Aunt Flo

Was like a dumpling on legs, with a face as gentle
With colour and wrinkles as a stored pippin,
Her flesh rich and as yeasty as fresh bread.
When she served dinner we would all rush
For the far end of the long table,
The plates passed down as she overwhelmed them
With potatoes, meat, gravy and greens
Until the dishes and tureens were empty.
'Oh dear,' she would say to those who sat near her,
'There's none left for you!'
Then the ritual was to be sent to the kitchen
                                    for cheese
And a cottage loaf which prompted me to wonder
Did the baker use her as a model?

Strictly teetotal she sustained her abstinence
On Wincarnis and home made wines.
'It's good for you,' she would say
To nephews and nieces, 'it's natural.'
While mothers winced to see their young ones
                                        reeling away,
And her more sophisticated daughters
Recoiled at her too obvious refusal
To wear underwear in warm weather.

Delectably dotty, Aunt Flo
Blundered beautifully through life
And taught us, when later,
In despair of making sense of things,
That it didn't matter.

John Cotton

about auntie rose & her diet

my auntie rose says
'no sugar for me
just a little artificial sweetener
in my cup of tea'

she says
'just half a slice
of that lovely cake.
it looks so nice'

so she eats one half slice
& another half slice
& another half slice
& another
& another
& another

& her eyes glaze.
i can almost see her
growing fatter & fatter
till the cake's all gone & then
she says 'oh well
it doesn't really matter
there's another one in the fridge
on a baked meringue platter'

when she's eaten that she laughs
she says 'my clothes don't fit me
any more' & we're off on the bus
to the larger ladies' fashion store

after that she says 'my word,
that's really worn me out
it must be lunchtime
my stomach's crying out for food'

in the coffee shop she says,
'i'm back on the diet
no sugar for me
just a little artificial sweetener
in my cup of tea

that dress i bought
is on the big side, so while we're here
let's have a pie
& half a slice of that lovely cake
it looks so nice . . .'

Jenny Boult

Uncle Fred

Uncle Fred with glares and stitches
Constantly repairs his britches.
Though he tries a larger fitting
Uncle Fred is always splitting,
Every straining seam expanding,
All his efforts notwithstanding.

Oh the ripping and the rending.
More repairs,alas, are pending.
Fat men who insist on bending
Can't expect a happy ending.

Max Fatchen

Visiting Auntie Mavis

'She's not got long to go,' said Mum,
'A week perhaps, her sister Muriel says.
She had it from the doctor
Who's been calling every day.
I've fixed for you to visit her tomorrow.
They've always been so good to you.'

Aunt Muriel let me in.
I've always called them aunties
Though they're not aunties really:
Just two kind old ladies
Who live next door but one.
The house so neat and hushed,
Flowers everywhere,
And Auntie Muriel almost whispering,
'She likes her visitors, but not for long:
About five minutes. After that she flops.'
We went upstairs, more flowers
On the landing, and in to
Auntie Mavis.
'Here's Annette for you, dear.
She's brought you primroses.'
And propped in pillows Auntie Mavis sat,
Her face caved in and pinchy
But all her make-up on
And her white hair lovely.
In her small voice: 'Hello, Annette.
It's like a florist's shop in here.
What lovely primroses. I remember
Picking posies just like that
From down by Donny's brook.'
And on she talked, asking
If my sprained ankle was better yet,
And was my brother Ted's
Engagement on or off and how
Was Dad and where were we going

For holidays: would it be Spain again?
I hardly said ten words,
Just answers, in that tidy room
With potted plants and bowls of fruit
And lime and orange juice.
And Auntie Mavis, like her sister said,
Tiring and out of words.
I thought her eyes were sad
And far away.
Then Auntie Muriel squeezed my elbow
And Auntie Mavis faintly said,
'Bye bye, Annette. Lovely to see you, dear.
Do come again.'

I cried a lot trying to tell Mum
How it went.
She just smiled and said,
'Weren't you a muggins then,
Letting her do all the talking.'

Eric Finney

My Uncle Ronnie

My uncle Ronnie
took me to Hackney Downs
and said:
how's your eyes?
how far can you see with your eyes?

So I said:
I can see that tree over there.
So he said:
Aha. But can you see the leaves on
        the tree over there?
and I said:
I can see that tree
I can see the leaves
on that tree over there.

All right, he says,
you say you can see the leaves
        on that tree.
Now, Mick, I'm telling you true
I can see a fly
sitting on a leaf
in that tree.
How about you?

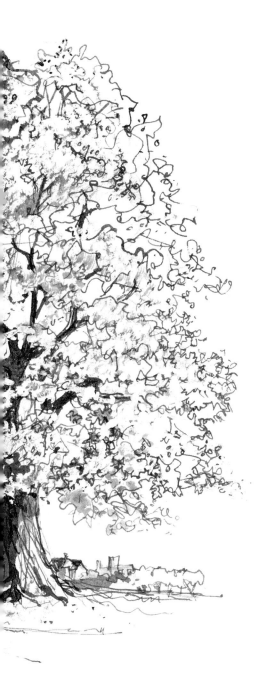

And I said:
I don't know.
I'm not sure.
Perhaps.
Maybe
Sort of.
Nearly.

Now, says my uncle Ron,
you see that tree
you see those leaves
you see that fly
well I tell you
I can see a leg
on that fly
on the leaf
on that tree over there
and what's more —
I can see a hair
on the leg of that fly
on the leaf on that tree over there
and —
Ronnie, I said, Uncle Ron
I can't see the hair on the leg
Uncle Ron, *I* can't see where the hair is.

The hair's on the knee, Mick
the hair's on the knee
Quick, look. Just there, quick.
Oh bad luck. You're too late.
The feller's gone and gone.

Michael Rosen

Uncle Tom

'I'll tell you what we'll do, boy,
Get two ponies, camping gear and food,
And travelling light, each night we'll camp
Where day's end finds us.
You'll like that the camp fires and the woods.'
And there's no doubt I would have done.

Often we talked of it,
My Uncle and I. He fresh faced,
With something of the countryman,
Though if he'd ever been such
I'm not sure. He could certainly ride well,
Sit a horse, I'll say that.
Learnt as a trooper in the cavalry.

Often I dreamed of it:
Lush lazy days beside a pony,
Sleeping under stars, and the bright mornings
Wonderfully fresh, the freedom and the air;

But they never came.
And, as in time, I knew they never would,
I didn't hold it against him,

Those promises, the hopes he raised.
Even now, the boy near two score on,
Uncle long dead, I occasionally remember
And gain some pleasure from it.

John Cotton

Acts of Love

It was my cousin Harry —
ungainly, slurred of speech —
who showed me love.
He used to take me down the yard —
'You come with me, my duck.' —
to see his budgies,
show off his prize-cards
pinned in a crooked patchwork round the shed.

Then he would coax his favourite from the cage
cupping her breathing emerald
in his familiar hand.
I watched his stubby finger stroke her head,
linger among the lapping coverts of her wings,
explore the underdown of breast,
gentle her brittle claws.
I stood, forgotten,
while they shared a shred of song.
His thick lips brushed her bill
murmuring 'There's my beauty, now.'
I ached for someone
who would whisper so to me.

Sheila Simmons

Uncle

Uncle was Gran's brother,
came to stay when she died,
kept to his room at the top of the stairs
but on Sundays he polished shoes.

Uncle was expert, a real shoe sheriff.
Each size ten had a price on its head
till he rounded it up with the rest.
He'd lasso Mum's boots and whistle
till plimsolls came running.
He knew, of course, where I threw mine,
when one was missing, he'd corner the dog,
then search through his bed till he found it.

The shoes submitted instantly:
they waited, trembling in line,
while one by one Uncle slapped on polish,
cleaned off the week's wear and tear
then buffed them to a shine.

He'd brighten the shabbiest pair,
the ones that had skulked for months
in a cupboard beneath the stairs.
He'd untangle loops and knots
then leave the shoes in rows,
till like some general inspecting troops
I'd signal which ones went back
for a second go.

When he died I took on his job
for a while, cleaned shoes for money.
I'd rub away like Aladdin and think
how my efforts might free Uncle's ghost.
I knew how much he'd be missing that mix
of polish and Sunday roast.

Brian Moses

Unfair

They say I've got my father's nose
They say I've got his walk
And there's something about my grandad
In the serious way I talk.

'And aren't his legs just like our Jack's,'
Says smiling Auntie Rose
'He could bend them just like that
And touch his head with his toes.'

I've got Auntie Julia's funny laugh
I've sister Betty's lips
And just like Sid on my mother's side
I'm fond of fish and chips.

I have moods that remind them of Auntie Vi
And my hair's just like their Paul
Sometimes when I look in the mirror
I wonder if I'm me at all.

But what I ask myself is this —
Why does it have to be
That it's me who looks like them and not
Them that looks like me.

Gareth Owen

Family Tree

I am
the family tree.
Before time barely had begun
I rooted,
splintering frozen stone.

I am
the family tree.
Through fire and ice I've crept and crawled,
roots stretching wider,
branches tall.

I am
the family tree.
Those roots, now laced in ancient moss,
still feed young branches
grasping into space.

I am their base;
I am your base.

Judith Nicholls

Index of Titles and First Lines

Acknowledgements

The editor and publisher are grateful for permission to include the following copyright material. Previously unpublished poems (© 1993) are reprinted by permission of the author unless otherwise stated.

John Agard, 'The Older the Violin the Sweeter the Tune' from *Say It Again Granny* (Bodley Head). Reprinted by permission of Random House UK Ltd. **Moira Andrew**, 'A Thoroughly Modern Grandma', © Moira Andrew 1993; 'Child with a Cause', published in *Go & Open the Door*, ed. Moira Andrew (1987); 'Tomorrow is Another Day', © Moira Andrew 1990. All reprinted by permission of the author. **James Berry**, 'Mum Dad and Me' and 'Listn Big Brodda Dread, Na!' from *When I Dance*, © James Berry 1988. Published by Hamish Hamilton Children's Books. Used with permission. **Valerie Bloom**, 'New Baby', © Valerie Bloom 1993. **John Bond**, 'When I was Your Age', © John Bond, 1993. **Jenny Boult**, 'about auntie rose and her diet'. Reprinted by permission of the author. **Tony Bradman**, 'The Picture' from *All Together Now!*, © Tony Bradman 1989. Published by Viking Kestrel, 1989. Used with permission. **Jacqueline Brown**, 'The Seven Commandments According to Mum', © Jacqueline Brown 1993. **Dave Calder,** 'in the cellar', © Dave Calder 1993. **John Coldwell**, 'My Dad Comes in all Shapes and Sizes' and 'Mum Doesn't Live with Us Any More', both © John Coldwell 1993. **Wendy Cope**, 'Cradle Song', © Wendy Cope 1993, and reprinted by permission of the author. 'Names' from *Serious Concerns*. Reprinted by permission of Faber & Faber Ltd. **John Cotton**, 'Aunt Flo', published in *Over the Bridge* (Puffin, 1981), © John Cotton 1981; 'Uncle Tom', © John Cotton 1983. Both reprinted by permission of the author. **Lynette Craig**, 'An Embarrassing Mum' and 'A Family Photo', both © Lynette Craig 1993. **David Crystal**, 'A Parents' and Teenagers' Alphabet Book', © David Crystal 1993. **Peter Dixon**, 'My Mum' and 'Allotment Rose', both © Peter Dixon 1993. **Berlie Doherty**, 'Daydreams' from *Walking on Air* by Berlie Doherty (Collins, 1993). Reprinted by permission of the publisher. **Max Fatchen**, 'Uncle Fred' from *A Paddock of Poems* published by Penguin Books Australia Ltd. in connection with Omnibus Books, © Max Fatchen 1987. Reprinted by permission of John Johnson (Authors' Agent) Ltd. 'Why is it?' from *Songs for my Dog and Other Stories*, © Max Fatchen 1980. First Published by Viking Kestrel; 'Oh, Brother!' from *Wry Rhymes for Troublesome Times*, © Max Fatchen 1983. First Published by Viking Kestrel. Both published by permission of the publisher. **Eric Finney**, 'Visiting Auntie Mavis', © Eric Finney 1993. **John Foster**, 'Sarah, My Sister, has Asthma',. 'Wait For Me', and 'Grandad', all © John Foster 1993 and reprinted by permission of the author. 'Why is it?' from *Four O'Clock Friday: original poems by John Foster*, © John Foster 1991. Reprinted by permission of Oxford University Press. **Nikki Giovanni**, 'Stars' from *Spin a Soft Black Song*, © 1971 by Nikki Giovanni. Reprinted by permission of Farrar Straus & Giroux Inc. **Eloise Greenfield**, 'Aunt Lavinia' from *Nathaniel Talking* (Black Butterfly Children's Books, New York). **Janet Greenyer**, 'Without Dad', © Janet Greenyer 1993. **Dorian Haarhoff**, 'Grandfather' from *My Drum – South African Poetry for Young People* (Hippogriff Press). **Anne Harvey**, 'Snaps', © Anne Harvey 1993. **Trevor Harvey**, 'And Who Gets Blamed?', © Trevor Harvey 1993. **Jo Hilton**, 'Patterned Ways' from *The Unsaid Goodnight*, ed. Phil Carradice. Reprinted by permission of the author. **Geoffrey Holloway**, 'Grandpa', © Geoffrey Holloway 1993. **Peter Thabit Jones**, 'Harry Pushed Her'. Reprinted by permission of the author.